ISBN 978-0-282-53148-5
PIBN 10855298

ical Microreproductions / Institut canadien de microreproductions historiques

1987

The Institute has attempted to obtain the best
original copy available for filming. Features of this
copy which may be bibliographically unique,
which may alter any of the images in the
reproduction, or which may significantly change
the usual method of filming, are checked below.

L'Institut
qu'il lui a
de cet ex
point de
une imag
modifica
sont indi

☐ Coloured covers/
Couverture de couleur

☐ Covers damaged/
Couverture endommagée

☐ Covers restored and/or laminated/
Couverture restaurée et/ou pelliculée

☐ Cover title missing/
Le titre de couverture manque

☐ Coloured maps/
Cartes géographiques en couleur

☐ Coloured ink (i.e. other than blue or black)/
Encre de couleur (i.e. autre que bleue ou noire)

☐ Coloured plates and/or illustrations/
Planches et/ou illustrations en couleur

☐ Bound with other material/
Relié avec d'autres documents

☐ Tight binding may cause shadows or distortion
along interior margin/
La reliure serrée peut causer de l'ombre ou de la
distortion le long de la marge intérieure

☐ Blank leaves added during restoration may
appear within the text. Whenever possible, these
have been omitted from filming/
Il se peut que certaines pages blanches ajoutées
lors d'une restauration apparaissent dans le texte,
mais, lorsque cela était possible, ces pages n'ont
pas été filmées.

☐ Col
Pag

☐ Pag
Pag

☐ Pag
Pag

☑ Pag
Pag

☐ Pag
Pag

☑ Sho
Tra

☐ Qua
Qua

☐ Incl
Com

☐ Only
Seul

☐ Pag
slips
ensu
Les
obsc
etc.
obte

L'exemplaire filmé fut reproduit grâce à la
générosité de:

Metropolitan Toronto Library
Canadian History Department

Les images suivantes ont été reproduites avec le
plus grand soin, compte tenu de la condition et
de la netteté de l'exemplaire filmé, et en
conformité avec les conditions du contrat de
filmage.

Les exemplaires originaux dont la couverture en
papier est imprimée sont filmés en commençant
par le premier plat et en terminant soit par la
dernière page qui comporte une empreinte
d'impression ou d'illustration, soit par le second
plat, selon le cas. Tous les autres exemplaires
originaux sont filmés en commençant par la
première page qui comporte une empreinte
d'impression ou d'illustration et en terminant par
la dernière page qui comporte une telle
empreinte.

Un des symboles suivants apparaîtra sur la
dernière image de chaque microfiche, selon le
cas: le symbole →signifie "A SUIVRE", le
symbole ▽ signifie "FIN".

Les cartes, planches, tableaux, etc., peuvent être
filmés à des taux de réduction différents.
Lorsque le document est trop grand pour être
reproduit en un seul cliché, il est filmé à partir
de l'angle supérieur gauche, de gauche à droite,
et de haut en bas, en prenant le nombre
d'images nécessaire. Les diagrammes suivants
illustrent la méthode.

3

1

OF THE

AWFUL DISCLOSURES

OF

MARIA MONK.

IN WHICH THE FACTS ARE FAIRLY STATED, AND CANDIDLY
EXAMINED.

——

BY G. VALE,

5-110

A REVIEW

OF THE

DISCLOSURES

OF

MARIA MONK.

We are informed by the Rev· Mr. Tappin, Chaplain to the
Alms House that there is such a person as Maria Monk, that
she came to this city last summer 1835: and we learn from her
work that she was then with child, as she says by Father
Phelin parish priest of Montreal: she was admitted into the
Aims House, and the child was born in the autumn of last year.
We learn too from the book, that Maria Monk related the substance of the contents of the book to Mr Tappin in the Alms
House; and that gentleman confirms this statement to us. We
learn also that, a Mr. William K. Hoyt, took Maria from out
of the Alms House, received her testimony and took her to
Canada, and represented her case to the British authorities
there; that these obtained a manuscript copy of her statements,
and now retain it, to forward we suppose to the head of the
Colonial Department in London, and then wait for instructions:
from that quarter we do not however expect any action, as
policy will govern the British Government. Mr Hoyt, it appears,
on his return prepared to publish this account, from a second
copy which he had preserved and applied to the Rev. Mr
Bourn and Dr. Brownlee for literary assistance; but Mr Hoyt
becoming jealous of his new associates, and fearing they meant
to rob him of the honour and profit of publishing, by procuring
from Maria Monk the facts of the story, suddenly transported
her out of their reach, and placed her as he thought in a seques-
tered spot near Bellevue: but Dr. Brownlee's son, by accident
or design, rode out in that direction and discovered the spot, but
was himself discovered, and his object being suspected, Mr Hoyt
again transported Maria Monk, and placed her somewhere in
Jersey, and we suppose hurried out the book, without further
assistance from those gentlemen; and this we believe to be the

history of the book published by Howe & Bates, in which however, the name of Hoyt is not mentioned. The copy right it appears is secured by one P. Gordon, and as far off as the District court of Massachusetts; and being thus secured by a person not well known in New York, and in another state, while the publishers where in this city, at first awaked our suspicion that all was not right: and we seriously doubted, if any such person existed as Maria Monk, or the persons to whom she refers in her book. From the Catholic Bishop of New York we first learned that there were such convents as those named by Maria, and that there was such a Bishop, and that such priests did exist as she names in connexion with the convent; thus confirming the ground work of Maria's story. We then visited the chaplain of the Alms House, and from him obtained the fact that the contents of the book accorded with what she had told him. He also related, or rather we extracted from him the facts we have given in relation to Mr Hoyt, Dr. Brownlee and the Rev. Mr. Bourn; the object of the latter gentlemen was to secure an interest to Maria Monk in the work; while he speaks also respectfully of Mr Hoyt, as deserving a remuneration for the expense and trouble he has been at in making public this affair. With the subject of the property we have nothing to do, nor do we know that our readers have : but we have to do with the contents of the book; and so has every person in the community.

This book then, contains the following facts : That there are three convents in adjacent buildings in Montreal, and a seminary very near the convents; these convents are the Congregational, the Black, and the Grey Nunneries; the first devoted to the education of girls; the second to the care of the sick, distributing bread and medicines; and the last for the benefit of the insane. The inmates are novices and nuns; the former may at any time leave the convent, and are only admitted to a part of the building; the nuns of the Black Nunnery never leave the building, but are admitted to all the rooms in the nunnery, and take oaths when they take the veil, which bind them to obedience to the priests; those of the Congregational nunnery go out, and form the teachers for a considerable district about the country.

Of the Black Nunnery we shall chiefly speak, for of that Maria was a Nun, and she informs us that in addition to the charitable object of the institution, that the nuns, about one hundred and eighty, were all prostitutes to the priests, about one hundred and fifty, including those for a large district, making the seminary in the neighborhood of the nunnery their home; that the decency of selection was not even observed, but that promiscuous intercourse was carried into effect by brutal force and cunning on the part of the priests, and generally by an unwilling consent on the part of the females, who are deceived on taking the veil, when they expect to lead a life of chastity; but after taking an oath to obey the priests in *all* things are immediately unceremoniously informed by the *Lady* Superior, that that oath extends to prostituting their persons if required by the priests, who being priests, cannot sin; and this is followed up by Maria informing us that on the very evening of her taking the veil, that Father Dufrene violated her person, and then two other priests, who treated her brutally; that Father Dufrene again visited her on the same evening, and continued with her till morning. She informs us too, that these things are done in the most brutalizing manner, corrupting the mind by the most extreme grossness; and when the females are shocked by such conduct, they are informed that they must consider it as the will of God, and that it is intended to mortify the flesh in them. The consequences of this extended sensuality, including *all* the priests and *all* the nuns in the Black Nunnery, is that a great many children are born in the year, and Maria seriously informs us that these are at first baptised and then murdered by strangulation, and privately buried or thrown into a deep hole in the cellar, into which quick-lime is thrown, and a fluid poured in to take off the smell, and destroy the body, bones and all. The nuns too, are murdered, if they resist the will of the priests, or are known to wish to escape; and Maria gives a minute account of one such murder, at which she assisted. She declares too, that there was nearly a uniform disappearance of an old nun with the appearance of a new one, thus implying that the old ones are murdered, leaving very few to die a natural death: even one Lady Superior was suddenly missing, and another appointed by the Bishop. Of the Bishop, whom she distinctly names, she declares that she let him in one night by a private door, and passage which led to the Superior's room, and that he lay with the Superior for that night, while Maria slept on a sofa in the same room. Priests frequently retire, Maria observes, into the Holy Retreat, supposed by the world for prayer and meditation; but which, Maria declares to be a pretence, and that in those cases they are diseased, and that in consequence of their disease, nuns are diseased also; and that when she left the convent, Father Tombau was in the Holy Retreat. Even the times of confession are said by Maria to be prostituted to voluptuousness; and that the priests corrupt the minds of young girls and novices at that period, by proposing questions, implying the grossest conduct, and by indulging in gross sensuality with nuns who go to confess alone into a room with them.

The Seminary, we remarked, is the receptacle of the priests all around the country, and from that place they visit the nunnery for the purposes now mentioned : Maria, too, assures us that a subterranean passage leads from the seminary to the nunnery, and that another leads from the Congregational Nunnery to the Black, and that nuns from the former establishment visit the other for improper purposes. Thus Maria makes the broad assertion that the whole establishment is a brothel for the priests, who indulge in gross sensuality and murder without compunction.

These facts, if true, cannot be too extensively circulated, and if false, the baseness of publishing them should be unmasked; especially as respectable names on both sides are connected with the publication, though no such name is attached to the book ; and if the truth be doubtful from the manner of getting up the book, then the simplicity of those who have assisted Maria in getting up the book, should be made manifest, and some other persons more competent should take up the subject, and produce such proofs of the above facts, if believed true, as would be incontrovertible.

THE GENERAL ASPECT.

Gross as the charge is, as made by Maria Monk, there is certainly a consistency in the whole; and therefore the probability is, that the whole is either true or false, with exception of individual cases : if all the priests are given to gross voluptuousness, then that spirit would be seen in their confessions of young girls, as explained by Maria : children would be born, and must be disposed of; while the fear of exposure would even suggest the murder of any one who should attempt to escape ; for one crime leads to another : but that the *old nuns* should be killed, or mysteriously disappear as young ones are introduced, exceeds credibility, at least at first sight; for if the idea was prevalent in the nunnery, surely the old nuns would seek to escape, and an exposure would have taken place long ago. In the case of the old nuns, the account exceeds that of any tale of the worst ages of the church, or when royal protestant and really interested commissioners had authority thoroughly to investiga e nunneries: the utmost extent of their reports was that they discovered *some* convents where the priests and nuns were wholly given up to voluptuousness : it was never pretended that all the nunneries were in this state; or that all the priests were thus corrupt; and never, as we recollect, that the old nuns were destroyed,—this is certainly a modern discovery.

We think it within the range of possibility that a whole community of priests, possessing single blessedness, in communion with women similarly situated,should corrupt the women,bound by oaths to obey in all things ; and we think a young priest so situated, frequently confessing a beautiful young nun similarly situated in a room where none dared to enter; that in most cases the natural passions would prevail over every other feeling, but that all the nuns should enter in ignorance of this state of things, and expecting the mortification of such passions, and the exercise of personal piety, that these should be immediately immersed into involuntary voluptuousness of the grossest kind, involving child-murder in anticipation, and that several of these should not make their escape and declare it to the world, is almost incredible ; especially as most of these young women are really very pious, and in sincerity take the veil; that such persons should so act, without frequent efforts to escape, greatly increases the incredibility.

There is indeed one view by which we may suppose the convent at montreal more corrupt than others ; and that is the fact, that _ _ _ _ _ _ _ _ with the French at a very corrupt period, and the _ _ _ _ _ _ 'ng into the hands of the British after the Reformati _ _ the purifying influence of those searching time. _ such transfer took place before the French Revo _ d also, the equally purifying effects of that great _ as a counter balance it is now under the protection _ rful and effective Protestant Government, surrounded by Protestants, (new colonist,) and a neighbour, the independant Protestant United States; thus affording means of protection to any individual who should make disclosures. The British Government often oppre s some for policy ; but they do afford complete protection to what are called their subjects, from injury by other subjects, however powerful : the Morgan murder, and the murders in the South, would not have been committed with impunity, under the powerful protection of the British Government. The Truth of the book however depends upon other circumstances ; thus—1. Is Maria Monk credible for facts, where her evidence could have no colateral support ? 2. What evidence does she offer in her power to obtain besides her own ? 3. Is there such an accordance between the several of parts of the detail, as to establish the presumption of truth ? In the absence of almost all external evidence we shall investigate the internal, by examining the above questions.

Is Maria Monk credible for facts where her evidence could have no colateral support.

After Maria had been as a novice in the nunnery for *four* or *five* years, (*averaged* 4½) she left the nunnery without leave, and became an assistant teacher in a common school. We shall now quote a part from the book itself.—

" While engaged in this manner, I became acquainted with a man who soon proposed marriage ; and young and ignorant of the world as I was, I heard his offers with favour. On consulting with my friend, she expressed a friendly interest for me, advised me against taking such a step, and especially as I knew little about the man, except that a report was circulated unfavourable to his character. Unfortunately I was not wise enough to listen to her advice, and hastily married. In a few weeks, I had occasion to repent of the step I had taken, as the report proved true—a report which I thought justified, and indeed required our seperation. After I had been in St. Denis about three months, finding myself thus situated, and not knowing what else to do, I determined to return to the Convent, and pursue my former intention of becoming a Black nun, could I gain admittance. Knowing the many inquiries that the Superior would make relative to me, during my absence before leaving St. Denis, I agreed with the lady with whom I had been associated as a teacher, (when she went to Montreal, which she did very frequently,) to say to the Lady Superior I had been under her protection during my absence, which would satisfy and stop further inqury as I was sensible, should they know I had been married, I should not gain admittance."

Thus we find Maria a married woman *for a few weeks*, without stating who is her husband, and what were the peculiar circumstances of her separation : and she distinctly informs us that she entered the convent under false pretences, previously arranged ; in which she induced her friend to act a part : and thus fixes upon herself the character of a *deliberate liar.* Her motive, too, for entering the convent is no higher than " not knowing what else to do" she does not appear to have been even in distress, and being on friendly terms with her late imployer, who even *lied* to serve her, we suppose she might have returned from her few week's marriage to her school again. By this means Maria procured admittance into the nunnery, for the third time, on which occasion she thus speaks.—

9

"The money usually required for the admission of novices had not been expected from me. I had been admitted the first time without any such requisition; but now I chose to pay it for my re-admission. I knew that she (the Superior) was able to dispense with such a demand as well in this as the former case, and she knew that I was not in possession of any thing like the sum she required.

But I was bent on paying to the Nunnery, and accustomed to receive the doctrine often repeated to me before that time, that when the advantage of the church was consulted, the steps taken were justifiable, let them be what they would, I therefore resolved to obtain money on false pretences, confident, that if all were known it would be far from displeasing the Superior. I went to the brigade major, and asked him to give me the money payable to my mother from her pension, which amount-to about thirty dollars, and without questioning my authority to receive it in her name, he gave me it.

From several of her friends I obtained small sums under the name of loans, so that altogether I had soon raised a number of pounds, with which I hastened to the Nunnery and deposited a part in the hands of the Superior. She received the money with evident satisfaction, though she must have known that I could not have obtained it honestly; and I was at once re-admitted as a novice."

Now unfortunately Maria Monk, establishes her character by this portion of her book we have extracted as a *thief*, extending her depredations to several of her friends, and undertaken deliberately for no very pressing object: Maria attempts to palliate this conduct by *asserting* that the Superior *must* have known the money dishonestly obtained, and, thus making her as bad as herself; but this is clearly the *assertion* of an acknowledged thief and liar: the Superior may be as bad as herself, we are not disposed to defend her, but the proof is certainly wanting. Maria in another paragraph insinuates that this conduct is agreeable to the religious doctrines or instructions she had received, and that if *all* were known it would "be far from displeasing the Superior." This we must remark, really savors of Protestant influence in getting up the book; it looks very much like a Protestant suggestion: we are not partial to Catholicism, but in moral honesty, Catholics appear on a level with others, varying like other people with circumstances. In pages 84 and 85, Maria shows that she was instructed in lying by the Superior, and that she voluntarily lied to deceive the friends of the Noviats, and in page 82 and 83, she shows that the priests instructed her in lying and in the distinction between a religious lie and a wicked lie : and in various parts of the work, she shows that she habitually lied, sometimes in conjunction with a nun called Jane Ray, and sometimes on her own account, for her own benefit. Now put together her mysterious few week's marriage, her deliberate deceptions, her obtaining money from several of her friends as well as her mother's pension by deception, her acknowledged habitual lying in the convent, and the little principal which induced her to enter that establishment on the third time, and the conclusions we must come to, is, that Maria Monk is a weak unprincipled woman whose single testimony cannot be depended on. We proceed now to the second questions.

What evidence does Maria offer, within her power, or that of her patrons, besides her own?

The answer is, none, from one end of the book to the other there is scarcely a single reference that is accessible, confirming any important point in the book; and yet there was the means of obtaining *some*, and if this some had been procured it would undoubtedly have led to other evid nce: if however no attempt has been made to support her testimony by other evidence, there are some indirect references, from which we glean a little, and which in the hands of an intelligent and diligent person, would have been the means of ferreting out the truth, if the truth was desired. In p. 224, Maria shows that Mr.Conroy the Catholic priest of this city, called on her in the Alms House, but that she declined to see him ; she declares he called several times, and that he waited once an hour in a room where she sometimes was, but still he never saw her; that finding she declined seeing him, he sent to her several messages by one or more Irish or other women, and among other things these messages contained the following, " That I (Maria) need not think to avoid him, for it would be impossible for me to do so. That I might conceal myself as well as I could, but I should be found and taken." He informed her too, " that he had received full power and authority over me (Maria) from the Superior of the Hotel Dieu Nunnery of Montreal." She says at length, that she agreed to see him in the presence of Mr. T. (Tap :n the chaplain) or Mr. S. " which however was not agreed to." She concludes by saying, that she heard that Mr.Conroy continued to visit the house: ' once,' she remarks, ' I had determ.ned to leave the institution, and go to the Sisters of Charity; but circumstances occurred which gave me time for further reflection; and I *was saved from the destruction to which I should have been exposed.*" The last line was marked in italics just as we have done. Now here we have an indirect reference; Mr. Conroy is mentioned, and Mr. Tappin referred to. We have not seen Mr. Conroy, we find it unnecessary, for we get *better* testimony. Mr. Tappin, the Chaplain, informed us that he believed the book true " except in the case of Mr. Conroy, that there were a *few* things said about him that were not correct; that Maria Monk was surrounded by a set of idle vagabond women, who to frighten her told her all manner of tales."

If these are not the exact words, they are the exact sense; and thus we find that the *only* fact we have the means of testing is a *lie!* in which Maria is supposed to have been deceived by a set of idle vagabond women; and this certainly suggests the possibility of her having been deceived in other parts, by perhaps a set of idle vagabond men. Mr. Tappin, too, tells us that Mr. Conroy never was there an hour, but that he called perhaps several times, and as she would not see him he declined calling: this precisely accords with the bishop's statement to us on the subject, and therefore we conclude this account correct; and Mr. Tappin's testimony extremely honorable to himself, whatever may be his opinions. When Mr. Hoyt went to Canada with Maria, he had a fine opportunity to test some points of importance, and these as we before observed, would necessarily lead to other discoveries: and if he neglected such an opportunity of strengthening her testimony, it satisfies us that either he dared not make the inquiry, or was incapable of getting up the work, with what assistance he got. In page 27, Maria relates that *a girl* told her of certain indecencies of a priest when at confession, she afterwards repeats, p. 29, that several young women told her similar stories, and that these agreed with her own experience : yet not one of these girls are named, who are not said or supposed to be nuns; and these could have been sought out, and this part of her testimony substantiated, and thus have rendered probable other parts, in connection with this fact. In p. 28, is the account of the murder of a young beautiful squaw, by a priest, who ran away, and whose bloody knife was found near the body; but the *name* of the girl is not given. In p. 113, is an account of a horrid and brutal murder of a young nun, St. Francis, who had been abused by some priests, and had imprudently spoken of escape, and determined not to yield to prostitution. This woman was murdered in the presence of Maria and a large body of nuns, the Bishop, Superior, and several priests : her friends had been informed that " she had died a glorious death, and some of her heavenly expressions were repeated:" yet St. Frances was well known to Miss Louise Bosquet, of St. Denis, the school mistress with whom Maria had lived : through her, Mr.Hoyt when in Canada, might have found her friends, who had been cheated; and they might have demanded a *legal* enquiry, under the protection of the British Government; and in this way the truth *must* have been confirmed : but Mr. Hoyt or Maria has given us no such information, and if each individual wants to test the truth, he must now go to Canada, and indict certain individuals belonging to the convent upon the testimony of Maria, an acknowledged liar and thief; but Mr. Hoyt could have done this for the whole community, and thus established the truth of his statements, and made his publication respectable : at the same time too and from the same people, Mr. Hoyt could have known the fact of her few week's marriage, and thus have tested other parts of her story. In page 165 Maria relates that the Superior cheated an old priest, a little in liquor, by imposing on him an old unsaleable ornament made in the house, and adds, ' WE all approved the ingenious device, and assisted in deceiving him:' the ornament was charged to his account, and he was obliged to have it. Now this priest is not named, but he was accessible to Mr. Hoyt, and as no man likes to be cheated, the facts could have been drawn from him, and then we might believe that a Superior who would cheat, and avail herself of the assistance of the nuns to assist in the cheat, that she might instruct young nuns to prostitute their persons : this would not have been positive evidence for other parts, but it would go far to render other parts probable. Mr. Hoyt too, might have had the child sworn to Father Phelin, parish priest of Montreal, and thus have brought the affair into court, and gradually have brought out the truth : or he might have seen the holy father privately, and if a liar in the case of Maria, he might have detected it, for liars do not make a very straight story when closly examined.

Now as Mr. Hoyt has done none of these things when he might have done some of them at least. We conclude that Maria has not snpported her testimony by any other, when from her character, such support was essential to the credibility of the work.

Is there such an accordance between the several parts of the detail as to establish the presumption of the truth.

We noticed in the former part, that Maria had given no reference to persons that were available; there is the same neglect of dates, for which indeed she partly accounts, when she says that in the nunnery dates were neglected, either by design or accident. If Maria is sincere and her narrative true, this omission of dates is very nnfortunate for her; but if she has

not told the truth, the omission of dates may be designed on
her part: but it is hard to conceal the truth, and Maria com-
mits herself on the subject of her age, if Mr. Tappin is correct
in his supposition. In page 20, she relates that she entered the
Catholic school or School of the Nunnery, at ten years of age.
In page 30, she relates that she left the school after two years,
at which time she must have been *twelve* ; and before this period she relates, p. 29, that she heard at confession words from
the mouths of priests, what she *cannot relate*, and experienced
treatment corresponding; and that other females experienced
the same. On leaving the nunnery, Maria informs us that she
soon became dissatisfied, especially with her home, the particulars of which are *not* explained, and she concludes, " While
*out of the nunnery I saw nothing of religion ; if I had I believe
I never should have thought of becoming a nun.*" This expres-
sion struck us on first reading, as not natural to Maria, brought
up a Catholic, and who did not a short time since, even after
the manuscript was written, acknowledge conversion. We
thought at first, and we think so now, that it savors of protestant influence, and thus partly deteriorates the work. Being
as she says *soon* dissatisfied, (without designating the exact
time,) she entered the Black Nunnery as a novice; after some
prudent delay, and caution on the part of the principals of the
Convent. Maria informs us, p. 43, that she left this convent
after a residence of about two and a half years; her expres-
sion as to time is this:—' After I had been a Novice four or
five years, *that is, from the time I commenced school at the Convent,* &c." that is, from the time she was ten years of age, and
hence she would be at the time of thus leaving the Black Nunnery, fourteen and a half, taking the average of *four or five
years.* Maria left the Nunnery, it appears, without leave or
notice : admitting that no opposition would have been made
to her departure, had she made her wish known. On thus leaving the Convent in disgust at the behaviour of some of the
nuns to her, she went to St. Denis, and resided at first as an assistant to a young lady, her friend, who kept a common school,
and while thus engaged, she married, as before related, before
she was fourteen and three quarters, for at that period she had
been married and separated from her husband, and returned
again to the Convent; as she remained at St. Denis only three
months altogether: we have before related how long she remained married. and what means she used to get into the Convent, and we now only notice it for the sake of the time. ' Not
knowing what else to do,' she says, she again entered the Nun
nery, and soon after took the veil, as if she were a maid, and

expecting to be devoted to chastity and religious duties, as she herself says. Now in the title page, we find that she was a nun two years, and this would make her not quite seventeen when she left the nunnery with child by Father Phelin, parish priest of Montreal, as she says. She was admitted into the Alms House, and delivered of a child last Autumn, as we were informed by Mr. and Mrs. Tappin, the chaplain and his lady; and Mr. Tappin informs us, that she was then, when in the Alms House, or when he was in the habit of seeing her, about twenty-five years old: now allowing that she was six months out of the convent before she was delivered, and that is the utmost she could be, for she left in horror of child-murder, as she says, (and she could not be sure of being with child more than six months before her delivery,) then her age would be taking the average only, and that in favor of her statement, she would then be *seventeen* years and a half at the time of her delivery, and now she would be about *eighteen*; but *Mr.* Tappin told us he thought her about twenty-five, and his lady sitting by and hearing the conversation, made no correction ; and therefore she would now be twenty-five and a half, an age much more agreeable to the nature of the narrative than that of seventeen and a half: but the two are incompatible. We have no interest in this inquiry, nor do we suffer any influence: we called on the Catholic Bishop, and we called on *Mr.* Tappin, as a stranger, and we left as we called, leaving in both cases our name, but without expressing either our faith or views, which indeed were not then definite, as we were only enquiring after the truth. *Mr.* Tappin may have been mistaken in the age of *Maria*, yet we asked more than once, but not so as to awaken any curiosity: we wanted to get the facts without awakening prejudice; and we believe we did; had he said eighteen, we should have published it: and we now give the fact as the means of testing the truth.

If *Maria* is now *eighteen*, it supports that part of her testimony which refers to the time of her acquaintance with the nunnery, and some of the transactions: if she is twenty-five and a half, it destroys a part of her evidence. Our object is truth, and this the means of testing it. We have seen in some periodicals lately, that she is estimated by appearance at about 20, by some who have just had a peep at her since her good fortune: the state of her feelings, her dress, and circumstances, will make some difference in the appearance of her age, and this may account for the different estimates : but the chaplain was her confidant, and was much with her, and the facts can be ascertained, and ought to be; and she herself ought to have made this matter clear, it was within her power.

In connection with her age are several facts: she must have been married at the early age of fourteen and a half, yet this unusual early age is not noticed: she must have become a nun between the ages of fourteen and fifteen or before she was fifteen; yet she does not notice the fact, although she even notices that the youngest girl entered as a nun was but *fourteen*; and when mentioning this fact we should expect a reference to her own age, which did not much exceed it. Of that young nun she says she *heard* she was much ill-used by the priests, and died in consequence. We can too scarcly conceive of the Lady Superior instructing a young girl of 14, or 15 years of age, in the practice of prostitution on her *first* taking the veil, as Maria asserts, in connexion with the fact, of the girl's being pious and sincere, and the institution a religious one; this conduct exceeds that of the most abandaned procuress or keeper of houses of ill fame that exist in the most corrupt and voluptuous cities in the Old World: yet the thing is possible. In Maria's case, who entered, not knowing what else to do, and after a *few* weeks marriage, the case might be different, and the effects different upon her; but the Superior was deceived, supposed her a virgin, and therefore we can scarcely credit this initiating instruction.

In page 62 Maria shows that on the day in which she took the veil Father Dufrene took her into a *"private* apartment and treated her in a brutal manner" two other priests afterwards did the same that evening, after which Father Dufrene returned and compelled her to pass the night with him. In Maria's discription of the nunnery she mentions *private* rooms appropriated to corruptions, and even at confession when in *private*, with the priest, while other nuns were outside each urging the other to go in first, because of the consequences; still the prostitution was in private; and this is the general idea preserved in the book; yet Maria mentions singular exceptions, which if true are not reconcileable with this general privacy of the practices referred to. In page 35 there is a description of the sleeping rooms of the novices: thus—

'The beds were placed in rows, without curtains or any thing else to obstruct the view; and in one corner was a small room part tioned off, in which was the bed of the night-watch, that is, the old nun that was appointed to oversee us for the night. In each side of the partition were two holes, through which she coul l look out upon us whenever she pleased. Her bed was a little raised above the level of the others. There was a lamp hung in the middle of our chamber showing every thing to her distinctly; and as she has no light in her little room, we never could perceive whether she was awake or asleep."

Now there is no deliberate description of the nuns bed room, but we learn indirectly that the apartment for the nuns is nearly the same: thus, in page 64, speaking of the nuns she thus proceeds:—

"On Thursday morning, the bell ruug at half-pass six to waken us. The old nun who was acting as night-watch immediately spoke aloud:

"Voici le Seigneur qui vient." (Behold the Lord cometh.) The nuns all responded:

"Allons—y devant lui." (Let us go and meet him.)

We then rose immediately, and dressed as expeditiously as possible, stepped into the passage-way at the foot of our beds as soon as we were ready, and taking places each beside her opposite companion. Thus we were soon drawn up in a double row the whole length of the room, with our hands folded across our breasts, and concealed in the broad cuffs of our sleeves. Not a word was uttered. When the signal · as given, we all proceeded to the community-room, which is spacious and took our places in rows facing the entrance, near which the Superior was seated in a vergiere."

After repeating the various ceremonies of the day, Maria concludes thus :—

"Standing near the door, we dipped our fingers in the holy water, crossed and blessed ourselves, and proceeded up to the sleeping room in the usual order; two by two. When we had got into bed, we repeated a prayer beginning with:

"Mon Dieu, je vous donne mon cœur,"

"My God, I give you my heart;"

and then an old nun, bringing some holy water, sprinkled it on our beds to drive away the devil, while we took some and crossed ourselves again.

At nine o'clock the bell rung, and all who were awake're-peated a prayer, called the offrande; those who were asleep were considered as excused."

Thus then it appears they slept in a body, a watch over them, and a light in the room; for the *watch* or guardian old nun, and the exercises, supposes a light in the nuns rooms as well as in the novices; the parties in bed too were to observe *silence.* Now Maria in page 145 after noticing the discovery of a secret passage leading from the Seminary, remarks, that she now saw how it was that priests appeared among them without her before knowing how they got in, and that they could "come up to the door of the Superior's room at any hour, then up the stairs into our sleeping room or where they chose. And often they were in our beds before us." We must here remember that the nuns slept in a public room, with a light and a watch; that they repeated prayers, and those who were awake, renewed their prayers one hour after they were in bed, and with the exception of these prayers were to keep silence : now, if this grossness were practised, which we can scarcely conceive common, even in brothels—if we can conceive of this public prostitution, in conjunction too with the ceremonies of the sleeping room; then we can see no necessity for any private or secret debauches; and yet the tenor of the book supposes, and expressly says, private apartments were the scenes of gross corruptions. Maria gives a fact in relation to this shameful publicity of prostitution, incompatible with the *secret* vice, and common prudence. She describes, p. 149, a young girl having taken the veil, and the name of St. Martin, sleeping on the first night nearly opposite to her, that she shrieked out in the night, and that she discovered the voice of Father Quiblier, and several nuns assured her that that priest was there: the Superior commanded audibly the young woman to obey. Now that any *experienced* priest should invade in a public room, the bed of a supposed maid, a pious girl, and not previously corrupted, except by the supposed recent instructions of the Superior, is improbable; for there was no possibility in public of his using successfully either persuasion or force; and that Father Quiblier, if he had really the experience ascribed to him, must have known. Lord Byron gets Don Juan into a situation something like that of Father Q.; but Don Juan's lady, was one of the Turkish harem, under restraint, with no religious feelings or recent vows of chastity; no previous bad spirits; and yet with all this difference, Byron does not make his hero succeed. Maria gives one other case of publicity, and on this occasion she selects noble game—the Bishop Latique and the Lady Superior. Maria shows that while she was one night attending on the Lady Superior, and sleeping in her room on a sofa, a bell was rung, leading from the street to the Superior's room : Maria was sent along the well known secret passage to answer the bell, when she heard the signal *hissing*, used by all the priests at any late hour; and this she answered by the usual ' Hum, hum,' and then let in Bishop Latique, who finding she was a *received*, that is a *nun*, directed her to conduct him to the Superior's apartment, which she did; he then " went to bed,' (with the su-

18

perior, we are left to suppose) ' drew the curtains behind him,
and I lay down on the sofa until morning, when the Superior
called me at an early hour, about day-light, and directed me to
show him (the Bishop,) the door." Now this Bishop story,be-
sides the grossness of sleeping with the Lady Superior, while
Maria was in the room, involves other peculiarities which must
be remembered. That any but a *received*, or a nun, should be
acquainted with the secret passage leading to the outer door, is
not to be supposed, and hence the Bishop asked a foolish question; but these apparently foolish things, serve to detect the
truth; the other inferences we shall leave for the present.

In page 73 and following pages Maria gives a minute description of the intererior of the building, and ascribes several rooms
to particular purposes ; among the rest, one for the nuns to give
birth to children in; another for priests deseased from sensuality ; and a third for nuns affected by the diseased priests ;
one for the baptism of infants before they are st.angled, and a
deep hole in the celler into which murdered bodies are thrown
on which quick lime and afterwards oil of vitriol is thrown: the
majority of the rooms however are for ordinary purposes. Maria
sets her credibility on this description of the apartments,and this
is a very weak point, for the discription of the room be correct,
except the purposes to which some of them are appropriated,
and yet the tale of infamy wrong . Maria's best evidence is her
being with child, if it can be clearly shown that she became
with child while a nun ; and that as a Black Nun she never left
the nunnery, while priests alone where the only men permitted
to visit her and other nuns: this is good evidence and what
she could have established to demonstration, if true: she could
have shown on what day she left the Nunnery, and that she was
with child at that time : and if the conductors of the Nunnery
could not show that she was turned out of the establishment
for getting with child, by a breach of some order, the inference
would be that the father of the child was a priest; and Father
Phelin might be he as well as any other. If Maria could not
recover dates while in the Nunnery, it is absurd to say she
could not remember the day she left it, and who she first saw,
and all the steps since till the birth of her child ; yes, you read
from the page 220 to the end about her leaving the Nunnery,
and coming to New York up to the present time with out a single reference. This fact we think condemns the book as false,
or the authors as men incapable of conceiving, collecting and
presenting the *proper* evidence for such important facts: Maria,
the publishers, and those who assisted her have only *said* she
was with child while a nun, and that none but priests had access
to the Nunnery: she had it in her power to prove it: she has not

done so, and thus rendered the story dependant on a thievish lying girl, without references which would establish her credibility even if a liar, and which references she might have given.

In page 93 Maria says that three or four days after she entered the Nunnery, she was sent for coal (charcoal) and she thus describes her perilous journey involving many awful particulars. This charcoal expedition, is we think one of the most extravagant statements in the book,for Maria does not say she lost her way she does not say that the dreadful hole which she discovered, was uncovered by accident, she does not say that it was unusual to have charcoal in so inconvenient a place; all is related as a common statement of facts, and these are her words :—

"Three or four days after my reception, the Superior sent me into the cellar for coal; after she had given me directions, I proceeded down a staircase, with a lamp in my hand. I soon found myself upon the bare earth, in a spacious place, so dark, that I could not at once distinguish its form, or size, but I observed that it had very solid stone walls, and was arched overhead, at no great elevation. Following my direction I proceeded onwards from the foot of the stairs, where appeared to be one end of the cellar. After walking about fifteen paces, I passed three small doors, on the right fastened with large iron bolts on the outside, pushed into posts of stone work, and each having a small opening above covered with a fine grating, secured by a smaller bolt. On my left, were three similar doors, resembling these, and placed opposite them.

Beyond these, the space became broader ; the doors evidently closed small compartments, projecting from the outer wall of the cellar. I soon stepped upon a wooden floor, on which were heaps of wool, coarse linen, and other articles, apparently deposited there for occasional use. I soon crossed the floor, and found the bare earth again under my feet.

A little further on, I found the cellar again contracted in size, by a row of closets, or smaller compartments projecting on each side. These were closed by doors of a different description from the first, having a simple fastening, and no opening through them.

Just beyond, on the left side, I passed a staircase leading up, and then three doors, much resembling those first discribed, standing opposite three more on the other side of the cellar. Having passed these, I found the cellar again enlarged as before, and here the earth appeared as if mixed with some whitish substance which attracted my attention.

As I proceeded, I found the whiteness increase, until the surface looked almost like snow, and in a short time I observed before me, a hole dug so deep into the earth that I could perceive no bottom. I stopped to observe it.—It was circular, perhaps twelve or fifteen feet across; in the middle of the cellar and unprotected by any kind of curb, so that one might easily have walked into it, in the dark.

The white substance which I had observed, was spread all over the surface around it; and lay in such quantity on all sides, that it seemed as if a great deal of it must have been thrown into the hole. It immediately occurred to me that the white substance was lime and that this must be the place where the infants where buried, after being murdered, as the Superior had informed me. I knew that the lime is often used by Roman Catholics in burying-places; and in this way I accounted for its being scattered about the spot in such quantities.

This was a shocking thought to me; but I can hardly tell how it affected me, as I had already been prepared to expect dreadful things in the Convent, and had undergone trials which prevented me from feeling as I should formerly have done in similar circumstances.

I passed the spot, therefore, with distressing thoughts, it is true, about the little corpses, which might be in that secret burying-place but with recollections also of the declarations which I had heard about the favour done their souls by sending them straight to heaven, and the necessary virtue accompanying all the actions of the priests.

Whether I noticed them or not, at the time, there is a window or two on each, nearly against the hole, in at which are sometimes thrown articles brought to them from without, for the use of the Convent. Through the window on my right, which opens into the yard, towards the cross street, lime is received from carts; and I then saw a large heap of it near the place.

Passing the hole, I came to a spot where was another projection on each side, with three cells like those I first described. Beyond them, in another broad part of the cellar, were heaps of vegetables, and other things: on the left, I found the charcoal I was in search of. This was placed in a heap against the wall, as I might then have observed, near a small high window, like the rest, at which it is thrown in. Beyond this spot, at a short distance, the cellar terminated·

The top quite to that point, is arched overhead, though at different heights, for the earth on the bottom is uneven, and in some places, several feet higher than in others.

Not liking to be alone in so spacious and gloomy a part of the

Convent, especially after the discovery, I hastened to return."

Now this extract is to us satisfactory: Charcoal for daily use never could be put in so inconvenient a place: the terrible hole in the floor never would be left uncovered. This hole, properly examined, serves to determine the whole question: the Catholic priests ought to submit this cellar to examination, and Maria, Mr. Hoyt, and others who have promoted this horrible Disclosure, ought to be obliged to promenade this cellar, and Maria ought to point out the spot where this hole is, or *was*, for if it be filled up, the *spot* will yet remain, and the filling up must be distinguished from the other parts which have not been disturbed: if this hole has not been disturbed, the contents at the bottom sho:;ld then be chemically and mechanically examined, and the remains of murdered humanity must be detected; for we find by an entry in a book, Maria says she discovered with Jane Ray, that every month affords a new supply to the amount of three or four children, besides the majority of old nuns, and murdered young ones, who may not submit to brutal force or voluntary prostitution : but if the bodies, bones and all, be decomposed, then the result, or compound substance will remain, and tell a tale as true; for there is no deception in chemistry ; and if the bottom be dug out or altered, a mechanical or close investigation will discover such alterations, and afford at least strong grounds for suspicion ; besides, the use to which this hole is applied, must be explained. This hole, then, affords the means of testing the truth of Maria Monk's and her assistant's story. Should it be found true, the guilty should be brought to justice and suffer the indignation of the public; and should it be proved false, Maria and her guilty partners should be made to feel the pains and penalties due to calumniators of the blackest die. As to the passage to the Seminary, and that to the Congregational Nunnery, these might be sought after too; but they would prove nothing material ; for these might exist like the general order of the apartments, and be harmless: the use to which they are alledged to be put, being only crimina .

The death of St. Frances, in the presence of the Bishop and the Superior, five priests and many nuns, including Maria, who took a part in it, as related in pages 114, 15, 16, 17, &c., is incredible; for why should it be so public ; people disposed to murder, seldom call witnesses, when the murder could be (qually well effected without it, and the *old nuns*, we are lei. , understand, are *quietly* murdered; whereas, Maria says, this St. Frances was gagged, thrown on a bed, covered by another, and that then the priests and nuns jumped on the bed with much satisfaction, till the victim was destroyed : the priest Bonin is distinguished in this transaction as most ferocious, and Father Richards is represented as wishing to save her.

Equally public are the children murdered, who are said to be strangled by the old nuns, after being baptised. Maria says she witnessed the death of the twins of St. Catharine, but one month after the death of St.Frances : and her presence appears accidental, as if no care was taken either to conceal or familiarize the nuns to these scenes. One of the nunneries, we remark too, took in *foundlings* ; surely some of the children said to be born in the Convent, might have found a safe assylum there, without recourse to uniform murder.

In p. 219, &c. Maria relates her escape, (without date, or whom she first saw as before related) she shows the difficulty she had to escape, and implies that nuns cannot get out if they would ; yet she shows in ano'her part before referred to, that priests come in at all hours in the night ; ring the bell leading to the Superior's room; that they make a hissing noise, and that the nuns let them in after replying by ' Hum, hum,' in order that they might not be deceived. She shows, too, that she actually let in the Bishop through this secret passage to the superior's room, and let him out again by the direction of the Superior. She had also access to all the rooms by her condition as a nun, and sometimes slept in the Superior's room, as on the very night she says the Bishop slept there: What difficulty was there then in letting herself out ? None, according to her own showing; and she and any other nun could go out at any time with very little contrivance ; just as easy as she could let in the Bishop and show him out.

If Maria was very young and not 25 or 26, as the Chaplin supposes, then there is an immense difficulty is her having a companion in Jane Ray, about 30 years of age : and in all her actions with that female, which supposes a person of maturer age, instead of a girl of fifteen or sixteen at most: her employments of reading to the novices &c. but ill comports with that early age, for many of the novices must then be her superiors in age,knowledge,and behaviour,as she does not represent herself as being extraord'i

Maria relates t uding a large di trict of
co crime of murder,
that *all*
the Con-
nunnery
es : now

would have repented and have disclosed the secrets of the establishment; but no disclosures have been made by them. The presta too enter on their studies young; and some come from abroad; and some are converted from other religions; some may no doubt be very wicked men, but that *all* should become debauchees and murderers is incredible: at what time are young and innocent students initiated; when are the foreigners introduced into these abominable corruptions? When are the *converts* made acquainted with these new evidences of the truth of this religion. Father Richards is well known in this city as a former Methodist preacher, and as a man of great humanity: he it was who wished to save St. Francis, and this fact has been pointed out to us by some respectable Methodist as proof of Maria's story: but if Father Richards was sincere in his conversion, and retains his humanity, and honesty, could he sanction child murder: could he sanction the murder the St. Francis by his consent, and after silence, even though he did apparently wish to save her; or is this assumption of his wish to save her put in to suit his former known character: and thus in reality sets him against himself. A Methodist preacher and humane man becomes a Canadian Catholic priest, and then practices adultery, and partakes in the murder of infants, refractory nuns, and old nuns, to make way for new ones, but yet retains his humanity, and wishes to save St. Francis: the thing is absurd: in the course of years there must have been *some* priests, who would have been conscience smitten, and have divulged the secrets: yet *no priest*, converted or not, has ever exposed the supposed inhumanity and corruptions.

Throughout Maria's book there is a marked Protestant tone and influence; concealed indeed as much as possible: we have no objection to Protestantism; indeed we prefer it to Catholicism in every form, but we must be impartial, and we must admit that there is throughout the book strong marks of Protestant influence and prejudice, which suggest the idea that those who assisted Maria were among that class who would *wish* the contents of her book true. Marks of this kind will be found on the title page, in the Scripture quotation; in page 59, where she says " being unaccustomed to *Protestant society*, she heard *no* appeal to the Bible," see also pages 20, 21, 25 and 26, and 31. In page 101 she says she did'nt know what I. H. S. means; this perhaps *was* the case, but that she should express it in the *prese* tense and not say that she had since learned it, from Mr. Ho,t, Dr. Brownlee or others assisting her in her book, shows a Protestant wish to prove Catholic ignorance; and an attempt to conceal the author of the suggestion: in 209 is the same spirit, she is made to say speaking of the liquid poured into the hole in the celler,

24

she " thinks the liquor was called vitriol or *some such name ;*" she adds it will penetrate flesh and even bones; now this *some such name,* can only be explained by a contracted wish to make out Catholic ignorance; as if any woman had never heard of oil of vitriol, by its common name, and know its costic properties. The marks throughout the book of Protestant influence are too numerous to note, for this the book itself must be seen.

We now notice again that the book accumulates *all* that has ever been said against the worst nunneries in the worst ages; and makes even additions to them. We do not however think it a reprint; this accumulation of crimes in' one nunnery, and that she should witness them all in two years, at a very young age, is a miracle.

We noticed also, that the book had no ostensible author, or responsible persons connected with it, but the publishers, who must make money, and could therefore afford the risk; Maria is irresponsible, from her character and situation , Mr. Hoyt has not put his name to it ; Dr. Brownlee and Mr. Bourne have not publicly acknowledged what assistance they rendered: Gordon, to whom the copy-right is secured, was paid as an agent, we learn from Maria's present friends; and he is to receive a small sum from each edition. Maria, too, was to receive $80 on every new edition of 1000, guaranteed by the Harper's. We have this from an attorney who saw the documont, and who concludes unfavorably of Maria, from her rude manners in prison, when she visited Hoyt there, and her familiarity with him. " Hoyt, what has that fellow Conger against you ; you know I have plenty of money; you shall not stay here an hour," were among her familiarities. Maria in distress, in the Alms House, and with child, has turned these untoward circnmstances to admirable account, with the assistance of Mr. Hoyt, who is not now in repute, even by Maria's friends. The Catholics should prove, if possible, where Maria was, if not in the Convent, or at once admit her residence ; the former may be difficult: but Maria should have sworn the child to Father Phelin, and made other individual charges, which must have brought on an examination ; and she should have given her history out of the Convent, as the means of tracing her to and from the Convent, and fixing the fact of her being with child while in the Black Nunnery. She has net done so ; we have therefore no confidence in her Narrative, in herself, Mr. Hoyt, Gordon, Dwight, the alledged editor, Mr.Bourne, or Dr. Brownlee, names unfortunately connected with strong prejudices against Catholics, and with most intolerant spirits.

name ;"
his *some*
to make
heard of
ɔperties.
ɪ are too

that has
st ages ;
er think
ɪry, and
ɪ young

thor, or
ɪrs, who
Maria
r. Hoyt
ne have
d : Gor-
ɪ agent,
ceive a
ive $80
's. We
ɪd who
ɪ in pri-
ith him.
know I
'," were
House,
ɪs to ad-
o is not
should
ɪent, or
ɪlt : but
d made
an ex-
ɪof the
ɔnvent,
ɪ Black
ɪ confi-
ɪwight,
unfor-
tholics,

---

y G. V.

SD - #0056 - 130722 - C0 - 229/152/2 - PB - 9780282531485 - Gloss Lamination